The Little Drummer Boy

illustrated by Yoshi Miyake

Troll

THE LITTLE DRUMMER BOY, by Katherine Davis, Henry Onorati, Harry Simeone
©1958 (Renewed) EMI Mills Music, Inc. and International Korwin Corp.
All Rights Reserved   Used by Permission
WARNER BROS. PUBLICATIONS U.S. INC., Miami, FL 33014

Illustrations copyright © 1998 by Yoshi Miyake.

Published by WhistleStop, an imprint and registered trademark of Troll
Communications L.L.C.

Printed in the United States of America.   ISBN: 0-8167-4809-8

10   9   8   7   6   5   4   3   2   1

To lay before the King
pa-rum pum pum pum
rum pum pum pum
rum pum pum pum,

I have no gift to bring
pa-rum pum pum pum,

That's fit to give our King
pa-rum pum pum pum
rum pum pum pum
rum pum pum pum,

I played my best for Him
pa-rum pum pum pum
rum pum pum pum
rum pum pum pum.

The Little Drummer Boy

Words and Music by KATHERINE DAVIS,
HENRY ONORATI, and HARRY SIMEONE

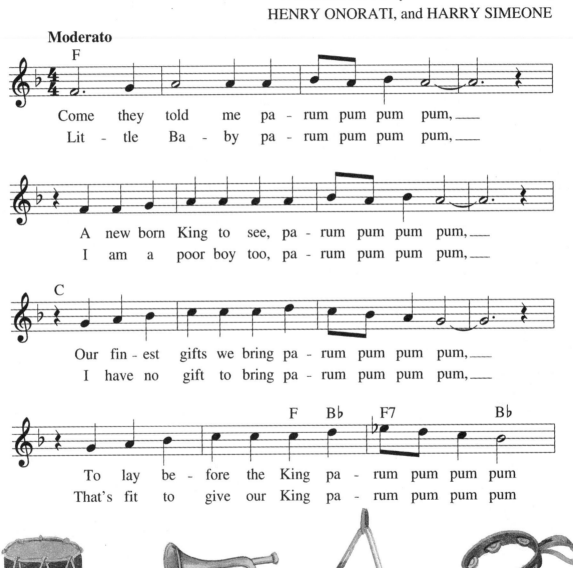